Requiem for a Dream

By Rachel Lawson

RACHEL LAWSON

As written on website AllPoetry.com http://allpoetry/The_Poette

Copyright 2021 Rachel Lawson

Requiem for a Dream

I grieve the loss of a dream,
I feel like from me tore a seam,
I lost my faith and hope with it,
I am lost sad and lonely I admit,
I fear life without the dream I bore,
I was happy in the light of my dream before,
I feel my dream has died,
I feel it to me had lied.
will you my dream just fade away,
disappear in an echo of pain one day as dreams do decay.

RACHEL LAWSON

Requiem for a Dream 2

I lament awaking from my dream sublime,
but all sleepers will wake in time,
I feel lost and alone without my dream,
I feel I am missing a vital seam,
I am like a tree broken at the stem,
all now of the dream I have is a requiem.

A Moon Shadow Nocturne

A play of light and dark,
under the wan light of the moon plays the skipping shadows of night's
dance their bewitching saraband with the moonlight,
silver moonlight and darkness melt into one in the cool airs of the
nocturnal bower of night,
the stars sparkle in the shadows far above the worldly cradle of man,
it is pure enchantment by moonlight,
a nocturne of moonlight and shadows melding it to one,
a song both dark and light with an ethereal heady air of enchantment
leaving the heart aglow

Yellow

I dream a dream so clear and mellow,
a soft sun glowing bright and yellow.
illuminating dawn dark and new,
the golden sun peeking out beneath the blue,
thick as golden honey,
smooth as fine held sand leaking from a hand runny,
the shadows drown in the sun's warm glow,
the world begins to Itself show.

as old parchments do the sands of the shores of dawn glow,
the daylight grows longer ever so slow,
like molten gold, the sky the day wakes up brighter,
chasing away the yellow stars of the night as it starts growing lighter,
the day has come bright as a morning can be,
the sky is blue and clear all can see,
the golden sun beats down warming heart and soul it did evoke
and then bathed in the light of the golden morn I awoke.

The Shadow of the Wind

Under the moon's silver glow
I heard the wind blow
the autumn leaves flew past me,
like charms in night's debris,
the wind it cools,
the night was full of the airs of scented jewels,
the breeze blew on the lake causing ripples of light and shadow,
I hear the wind's cries and see its tears which fly and show,
as crystalline glowing rain, it is the coming of a storm,
the shadows of the wind do form,
where the shadow of the wind does go
the aura of night shows in its glow.

Nocturne or the music of the night : Extended

The night is like music it is cool and crisp,
smooth and elegant,
the stars twinkle like music,
the moon sails across the sky like a music score,
the darkness is the beat of the heart listening to music or looking in the
mystery which is the night,
the night enthrals like a sweet riff of music,
the beauty of the night is the music of the stars,
the ghostly light of night is like an aria soft,
a song of the night is the unearthly glow,
the ethereal atmosphere of the night is like a favourite song,
night tugs on the heartstrings like a beautiful voice in song,
it is the music of the night

The Marvellous Light

Crystalline pure silvery aura of night,
is within my sight,
the moon glows full and bright,
it is a marvellous light.

The air is of silver and pearl, the night is liquid with moonlight- extended

The stars are silver diamonds placed upon a black velvet sky,
the leaves in the wind are gems floating in the cool crisp air,
the rain is falling stars like glowing diamonds,
the river is crystalline rippling mercury beneath the full moon's light,
the night is full of the sounds of life,
crickets chirp, frogs croak, night birds sing their sweet serenade of night,
my boat cuts through the river with a soft swish of water,
an ethereal glowing fog is hiding the river in patches,
the air is full of the scents of flowers on the shore,
the moon is like the gem moonstone bright and clear peaking out of
the clouds are shadowy faintly glowing cotton candy mist,
"The air is of silver and pearl, the night is liquid with moonlight."
I am breathless.

Like a Moth to a Flame

Humans chase the sun like a moth to a flame,
we rise with the sun and hibernated when the sun leaves,
We adore her sister the moon who is lit by the sun's loving glow,
The sun warms our hearts in our Earthly bower.

When We Were Young

When we were young the world was magical,
When we were young we were immortal,
When we were young the world was ours,
When we were young we could do anything,
When we were young our dream would all come true,
When we were young nothing could stop us,
When we were young love would find us,
When we were young anything was possible,
When we were young the world was a dream,
When we were young the world was our pearl,
When we were young fantasy was real,
When we were young we were all swashbuckling heroes,
When we were young no one could stop us,
When we were young we were dreamers,
When we were young romance was real,
When we were young there was always a happy ending.

In My Life

I have lived a life in dreams,
not all is as it seems,
everything is running as theme,
it's a lovely dream,
melting into a pool of happiness and pain,
like a bittersweet refrain,
sang by a melancholy singer in a song so sweet,
I know the future I will meet,
with similar heartfelt empathy as I do the past,
all comes and goes until days last.

A Thousand Million Eyes

They say the night has a thousand eyes,
That "One could not count the moons that shimmer on her roofs, or
the thousand splendid suns that hide behind her wall."
Beautiful sparkling eyes of stars the lonely travelers of the skies,
thy light charms all,
thy fires eternally burn,
the silvery beams from moons and suns illuminate the night with
night's alluring glow
the light of these hundred million suns and moons illuminate lovers
perpetual yearn,
they are distant and far memories of days eons ago.

The Reign of Rain

Cool and softly falls the rain,
from the silvery sky,
it comes sweetly hissing on my roof,
refreshing the world with its life-giving nectar.

RACHEL LAWSON

Saturn

Rings and diamonds,
a precious gem of space,
planet of ice and rock,
pressure under beauty,
diamonds melting into crystalline liquid diamonds in death.

Time Travel

I am a time traveler, as are we all, we travel through time moment by moment, the possibility of time and chance are considered possible in parallel universes, we all live on in this universal life, balancing upon the tightrope which is time and choice, controlling in which parallel world within which we live and die.

RACHEL LAWSON

The Mystery of Night

They say the night has a thousand Eyes,
It's beauty no one denies,
The nocturnal passing is cool and crisp,
The mind creates ghosts from a single wisp,
No man knows night truly,
Man knows it comes by dark and cooly,
It has a feeling of enchantment,
Beholders are usually lost in the moment,
The glazed eye that is the moon comes ever slowly,
In the dark speckled sky, people watch them longingly,
As they float by in night's procession,
They travel by with great precision,
Til wthe dawn time chorus comes,
And the day It becomes.

Let it snow

Softly falls the snow,
making hearts aglow,
cool crisp,
floating in a wisp.

RACHEL LAWSON

Wildflowers

Common some call them,
I am charmed by their wild exotic beauty,
they are to me dear to my heart,
they are elegant delicate beauties of nature,
although some call them weed,
but one man's weed is another's flower,

The Rose of Snow

Once existed a pure white rose,
from the snow, it rose,
a rose of purest snow,
from the snow, it did grow,
and by the snow, it did die,
in death, it was petals in the snow it did lie.

The Sea of Blue

I see a sea of blue,
a floral ocean of a single hue,
beneath a sky azure painted with fluffy clouds,
I am alone and breathless in these crowds,
the flowers are like water hugging the ground,
ever so enchanting blue above and blue, below blue all around,
I am drowning in this sea of blue,
it is the most intoxicating brew,
I drink in with my eyes this beauty,
I am light and heady,
I'm in heaven on Earth,
the beauty is beyond worth,
it is like a sea of cut aquamarine,
the sky is blue cloudy turquoise, no bluest tourmaline,
oh my, it is so enchanting I can barely speak,
I can not find more words I am speechless and I feel weak.

Liquid Gold

smoother than honey,
like a golden sunset sunny,
rich as glowing golden honey,
thick and runny
worth more than money.

Silver

Shiny metal of liquid white,
attractive and light,
natures gift to man,
posses it if you can,
it possesses you,
you, it does subdue.

The Eyes of Night

They say the night has a thousand eyes,
not many know the hows or whys,
they are the stars of light,
they are a beautiful sight,
they are the burning embers of stars long past,
they are the eyes of the night to their last,
when they close their eyes in fire or ice,
till their ends, someone always says it nice,

Death's Token

Upon my grave do not grieve,
Just leave upon it death's token in reprieve,
A single lily fear not my grave be not chilly,
It is the home of love I am now in heaven far above.

New Ways To Dream

I dream and see any thing can be,
It is a new way to dream for me,
I dream I can do anything,
I am so happy I feel like I can sing,
I could dance I feel high,
People ask me why?
I know my dream to them impossible does seem,
But I have found new ways to dream.

RACHEL LAWSON

Moonlight on the Water

A sparkling river cool and clear,
enchanted by nature's beauty divine,
pure elegance to the eye and mind.

In The Moonlight Hour

Stillness,
silence,
a cool air,
a silvery glow all around,
pure beauty,
darkness cut by moonlight and starlight.

RACHEL LAWSON

Thoughts

Life and death all come and go slow and fast,
sad and happy they are,
things come and go,
where will I go? When will I come?

The Night Is Like A Beautiful Gem

The stars are silver sparkling gems floating in the onyx sea of pitch,
the moon like an illuminated glowing gem moonstone that swims
through the starlit sky,
the air is cool and misty upon the lake tonight,
the ground sparkles with its frosty carpet,
the night is like a beautiful gem tonight.

RACHEL LAWSON

Dreaming

A fantasy world is dreaming,
beyond wakeful deeming,
nothing is as it should be,
nothing is beyond what you can see,
floating through the air,
without a worry or care,
that is all in a dream,
nothing is what it may seem.

The Blue Rose of Egypt

The blue lotus of the Nile,
it is a beauty there is no denial,
drug of the ancients,
its flower bloom requires patience,
it blooms but one time only,
the rose of Egypt bloom is lonely.

RACHEL LAWSON

Under the dust of the past lie, the days gone by

Under the dust of the past lie, the days gone by
lost in the shadows of time is where the dreams of the past do die,
from the night comes the new days to come,
it is from the dust the grows the world as it will become.

The Dark Side of the Hourglass

The sands in the hourglass creep by briskly,
with the sands fall lives and times and eras,
swift death comes when the sands of life's glass flow of sand stops,
it brings ends to lives, times and all thing within their sands stream
draw to it's end.

RACHEL LAWSON

The Eternal Flame

I burn with hope like an eternal flame,
the flame ignites a burning bright light,
I see things that never have been seen before,
the fire crackles and illuminates the mind,
the light awakens the soul to new things.

Sky Diamonds

Diamonds made of air,
Too precious to share,
Diamonds made by man,
Made only as scientists and dreamers can.

RACHEL LAWSON

The King of the Road

Upon the road, Dick Turpin met Tom, the King of the road,
he took Gentleman Tom as a fat pigeon,
as highwaymen in Epping Forest they rode,
Tom taught the code of the highway to Turpin,
it was Tom King who made Dick Turpin a legend,
"Your money or your life" they told anyone unlucky enough to be their
beholder,
Turpin it is rumoured was Tom King's end,
Tom was shot through the shoulder,
and was taken to see a surgeon,
they could not save him,
the guilt of killing Tom, was Turpin's burden,
Turpin's end was more strange and grim,
Dick gave up the road,
and became a butcher,
still, at night, he rode,
and was caught as a poacher,
Turpin wrote to his brother-in-law to get him out of jail,
at the jail, his old schoolmaster who had taught him saw the letter, in
an act like treason,
Turpin's teacher conspired a betrayal,
it wasn't Turpin's lucky season,
the teacher named the letter's writer,
Turpin was caught,
now he could not get help from his in-law brother,
for his crimes he ended his days at the end of a gallows knot.

Ghost Light

By ghost light, the lonely stage is lit,
no one is there it is lit for ghosts alone,
all of the actors are hiding from the stage,
people in crowds are shunned,
the era is one of fear,
so no one even there comes near,
only the ghost of productions past are there.

RACHEL LAWSON

A Nodding field of Crocuses

I stand in a field of Autumn Crocuses,
bobbing in the strong autumn wind,
I see a few grasshoppers or were they locusts,
whatever it is it is just in the viewer's mind.

The Veil of Night

Beneath the cool dark veil of the night,
a single candle cut through the night's shadows with light,
walking down a darkened park a nervous traveler strode down its small road,
suddenly a shadow moved in in the light into sight,
the traveler panicked and was struck by fright,
The shadow was a man in black on a horse a highwayman,
not your regular cut-purse,
"Your Money or your Life?" not wanting strife the traveler handed over their purse to the bandit,
the bandit true to his word rode off into the dark shadows of night,
the traveler timidly traveled on in full flight.

Catching Stars

The night is lonely and cold,
I wanted to do this before I get old,
I am a star hunter that's what I do,
I hunt for stars until the night is through,
with my net of night,
I catch their light,
I put it in jars like fireflies,
for me to go back on the hunt the night cries.

The Song of the Wheat Field

I stand amid a golden wheat field,
the wind blows the wheat which bends and folds,
so sweetly waving,
the breeze blowing through the wheat,
makes the wheat start to sing.
it sings long sad arias like mournful sighs.

Who Wants To Live Forever

Who wants to live forever,
who wants to die never,
who wants their world to never end in fatality,
who could take immortality?
who could stay sane,
who could take the pain,
who could take the loss of all they love,
who could but dream of heaven above,
who could take the aeons in their stride,
who could just sit and take the eternal ride,
who could not go mad,
who could not be sad,
who would want to see life wane,
who could have hope seeing the fade of life's chain,
who would go on smiling boldly,
who would not end up acting coldly,
Who wants to live forever,
who wants to die never,
who wants their world to never end in fatality,
who could take immortality?

Dreams

Words are the dreams the heart makes,
They are the wishes of the mind,
They are the heartaches and sighs,
They are the breaths and cries,
They are the life and end,
The light and dark,
They are the beauty of the night,
The warmth of the day,
The visions of the heart made real.

RACHEL LAWSON

Dusk To Dawn

The eventide brings with it the coldest hours
the daylight the night devours,
cold and wan the light does grow,
the sun goes to its roost leaving in her place the moon and stars aglow,
in her silvery bower,
the moon rules the night it is her hour,
when the dawn comes to the silver realm,
the night is no longer at the helm,
the night burns away,
into the golden light of day.

Water Color

Upon a lake swam 2 perfect snow-white birds,
the scene in whole was beyond words,
the water was stained with the colors of the autumnal trees nearby,
like a rainbow of color, the trees seemed to reach to the sky,
the dear little swans appeared oblivious to the beauty,
they swam about as if it was their duty.

RACHEL LAWSON

Moon Rise

The moon rises from a dark burning sea,
ink black clouds like smoke float between it and me,
the land is as dark as the night sky,
the clouds like smoke over the fiery water float by.

Dust of Eternity

The past is the dust of eternity,
it draws out all of memory,
it is the shadow of known time,
the sands of the hourglass fallen,
long is time on reverse looking back,
beyond the sands fallen is the future,
the sands waiting to fall.

RACHEL LAWSON

Reflections of Night

Sparkling jewels upon the water,
Come to my feverish mind,
Ethereal and Enchanting like a lovers song,
Heady yet delicate like a mist at sea,
Glowing like my arduous heart,
A sight never to be forgot,
Lighting the night with their faint iridescence,
Dying with the dawn's light.

The Dark Mystery of Night

It is a play of light and dark,
illuminated by a silvery spark,
what lies hidden out of sight,
it is the dark mystery which is the night.

RACHEL LAWSON

The Night's Lullaby

Night has come darkness is enfolding its wings around the earth,
the world falls silently to sleep under the lullaby of the sparkling stars
in the sky, while the song of the moon illuminates the world of night.

Dance of the Grinches

Bah Humbug! It's Christmas time,
When sensible people lose all their money it's winter time,
hate winter the ice and snow,
the houses a glow,
The no parking,
the people sing,
The traffic jams
the hams,
the empty stores,
the wreaths on doors.

Superb Blue Wren

Sweet and cute is the blue wren,
hopping about the bushes in the park,
happily chirping it's sweet pleasant song
as it goes on it's way.

Fire in the Sky

Like liquid white fire was the meteoric deluge,
like falling starlight on the starry night sky,
like glowing rain falling through the dark sky,
enchanting the heart and mind charming the very soul,
with every falling star.

Castles in the sky

Nothing is what it seems,
nothing is what the dreamer dreams,
they dream of lands a far,
they are never what they think they are,
they are just castles in the sky,
but for their dream the dreamer see pure and perfect place but if they
go there the dream would die.

I have not gone to war in order to collect cheese and eggs, but for another purpose

The Red Baron was a complex man,
he fought for his land like any soldier captain,
he was a man of valor,
he respected the men who he was fighting at war,
he made tributes for his victims lives
he died to save one of his relatives,

RACHEL LAWSON

The Death of the Red Baron

Twas a morn in April that the Baron Red from the sky did fall,
his cousin a fighter pilot was under attack he knew not what would befall,
the red baron came to his rescue swiftly,
he fought well for a while hereby,
until a bullet from the blue shattered his chest dying he did land nearby,
from where the bullet came was never fully explained,
but from his exploits and his death fame he gained.

The Mad Hatter

A cup of tea for you,
half a cup for me,
life is impossible without a good cup of tea,
on this unbirthday or any other,
so grab a cup and drink

RACHEL LAWSON

Even the whitest rose has a dark shadow

Even the purest rose of snow-white crisp and clear has a heart of darkness,
cut from its mother the rose bush as it commonly is,
it is the corpse of beauty it will become a corpse in time,
it's is nothing but a dying rose,
a picture of beauty in death.

Somewhere in Space

I exist somewhere in space,

I am stuck in time and place,
lost in the Milkyway's grace,
I follow times sweet pace,
I am within the Earth's worldly encase,
with a world of others I see and their face,
many see of this world a disgrace,
others see of it in a way to displace,
some see that we human do nothing but deface,
this world is with all its life is interlace,
life does not the earth debase,
life is in this world's embrace,
yourself please brace,
we don't the world efface,
nor this world can we erase,
such thoughts are mostly thoughts of misplace.

Seven Pillars of Wisdom

"The Lord is my light." he guided me all my life,
he guided me from birth and through my strife,
a Prince of men known and admired by all who I call a friend,
I travelled to Arabia where which I alone defend,
I helped free Damascus from the Ottoman Turk,
although some say I went berserk,
a free Arabia was always my dream,
after the war, I was accused of going Arab or to them it did seem,
I returned to real life and tried to hide,
my legend had grown too much for me to abide,
I could not be me!
Although the world could not see,
one day I rode hell for leather on my motorcycle near Clouds Hill my home,
I had a serious accident no longer did I roam,
I died and upon my grave, they wrote "Dominus illuminatio mea,"
"The Lord is my light." by those words my life did adhere.

RACHEL LAWSON

The History of the Universe

All was night,
till there came light,
from them came time,
times ascent in the dark a climb,
from time, light darkness came matter,
from matter and time started life in the batter,
time killed matter, light and life,
like all it ends in strife,
life, matter a light all in time end,
leaving nothing but night to ascend.

The Edge of Night

In the beginning, there was night,
then cutting through the darkness came a light,
and from it burst time,
from the primordial soup grew matter ringing like a chime,
then aeons later sprung life from light and matter,
matter and life, time did batter,
life, matter a light all in time end,
leaving nothing but night to ascend.

Night the Dark and Sparkling Traveler

The night is the silent traveler,
it is day's sweet unraveler,
it comes with charm and beauty the night's treasure,
the cool crispness in the dark's kiss of silver enchantment its lure
her sparkling eyes look down on the world as it sleeps,
in dawn's pale light she leaves,
the waking world grieves.

Sunset to sunrise

I love the time after the moon does rise,
the hours of day's goodbyes,
illuminated skies of pinks and peach glow warm and clear,
night comes like a sparkling chandelier,
in the cool dark velvet skies of night,
the moon the lonely friend shines silver and bright,
in the chilly crisp air, night birds sing and fly,
in the sacred stillness, all the world in sleep does lie,
the peace is like a sparkling wine only disturbed by the coming of the
dawn,
with the faint glow of morn's first light, the night is withdrawn.

RACHEL LAWSON

Night

Dark and cool,
clear and crisp,
your heart is hard to see,
your silver aura the heart inspires,
beauty is in the observer's eye,
you bear an air of enchantment,
Night comes to bewitch the soul,
the sparkling stars are like a glass of good champagne,
pure and clear is thy nocturnal glow,
like a ballad thy beauty,
the moon is exquisite in its charm and light,
the night is the jewel of the day.

Rendezvous with Moonlight

I have a rendezvous with moonlight,
it is a serenade of reverie and light,
the sands of the hourglass fall on like the snow it floats softly to my nose
my heart is warmed
I am as a spirit transformed,
Time slows and the world is like a fairies realm,
all is silent, the snow crunches underfoot the silver dream of night's
ethereal beauty at the helm,
I see my breath billow in the snow dancing sweetly in the night's glow,
the frozen lake shimmers like glass as I sit watching the stars and the
moon peeking through the clouds of snow,
the moon is like a smiling Cheshire cat in the sky in it is an owl in flight,
I am intoxicated by the beauty of the night.

RACHEL LAWSON

The End of Time

all things come to an end,
lives, eras eons memory,
even time its self with a final flailing
tick, tock, tick, tock,
and anything beyond it is none existence and silence and nothingness.

The Catacomb of the Heart

We all lose someone,
we all know death,
their loss brings pain,
the dead remain in the catacomb of the heart
for the rest of life's breath

RACHEL LAWSON

Life and Death

Life is short,
death is long,
live your life,
for death will come,
removing life's sweet breath.

A Blood Red Rose

Scarlet red,
the color of blood,
kissed by the crimson rose,
the heart's blood burns,
like Earth fire hot,
crystalline ruby liquid drips from the thorn pricked
finger of my love,
with the beauty of a blood rose,

RACHEL LAWSON

The Ethereal Magic of Words

Words can capture the very soul,
with their magic, they can enthrall,
sometimes a single word can be as inviting as a mermaid song,
words can inspire the heart to fly,
words can make you cry,
word spells the heart weaves

My Rose Lies Bleeding

My rose lies black and bleeding,
red blood from it does drip,
I fear it is in deaths cold clasp,
lost to this world in the graves dark embrace.

RACHEL LAWSON

The Power of Words

The crystalline essence of words is rich and syrupy,
clear and crisp,
strong and smooth,
dare you find the light in the darkness,
that illuminates the night with words purity and glow.

Sands of the Hourglass

Sand slips away in the hourglass,
drawing time with it,
bringing ages and eons with the sand fall,
til the sand runs out at the end of time.

I Am A Writer

Words burn in my soul,
words pour out of my mind beyond my control,
I write not for anyone or any goal,
my words are me,
they are the best I can see,
I trained in my craft young,
words come naturally to me.

A Bleak Winters Night

Dark and dreary,
cold and freezy,
grey clouds trace their ways across the winter night,
the cheery stars are hidden from sight,
the nights are more severe,
dreams of summer are dear,
all is bleak,
the warmth of the house we seek.

RACHEL LAWSON

Upon the dark waters

An old ship sails this glassy sea
follows the light-trail of the full moon
towards the hazy violet of the fading horizon
the sky has a hazy violet pink horizon above a starless sky,
her masts and hull silhouetted against the sky and melting in the sea.

The Beauty of Spirng

Little spring showers come,
blossoms of heaven scent are here,
sweet jonquil blooms with an air of ecstasy,
trees leaves are growing strong and green,
animal know the spring has come,
the heart skips and leaps into the flowers.

Forever Autumn

I am trapped in a world of Autumn,
the season of the fall,
leaves of rainbow colors do fall,
skies of deepest blue,
strong winds blow the leaves in the trees,
the leaves float through the sky like feathers in the wind,
the leaves fall in deep rainbow colored carpets.
its beauty will remain forever in my mind.

The River of Light

I hear a river washing upon the shores,
I see a river of light washing through the night's shore,
They wash is softly in the night which seems their home,
the night is dark and starlight as seen from my window,
the moon a plate of shining silver snow hanging in the sky like a
diamond bright,
the crystalline river is the light of many a car on the road driving in a
line,
the waves sound is the sound of car engines revving,
It is a modern river of night.

Wispy white cotton candy clouds

Wispy white cotton candy clouds sail upon a sky of zenith blue,
flying over fields of green,
the clouds turn grey and water the fields below,
they skip over oceans, rivers, and seas, in the breeze,
float over cities and towns,
like waves, they blow over deserts dry,
raining down on forests and tropics hard,
they are hard things clouds know,
plane above and through them fly,
clouds feed tree and grass with rain,
rain freezes into snow and coarse frozen hail,
there are many types of clouds,
tempestuous storm,
fluffy non-rain clouds,
clouds like paintings,
grayish tinged rain clouds,
others look like waves in the sea,
people see in them images of things,
which aren't there,
still more try to predict them,
and some do fail,
clouds are amazing things.

A Peacful Scene

A graceful yellow and pink rimed peace rose did grow in a patch of
buttercups by a river,
nearby was a steaming waterfall down a rocky cliff,
below it a green grass shore,
the sun was waning the clouds bars they glowed yellow and orange
above night showed a bar in night's dark shade.

RACHEL LAWSON

The River Has No End

Water, water as far as I can see,,
Is it true that the river has no end,
Can it be?
The eternal flow rolls forever more,
From the land to the sea,
Beyond the rivers flow it flows evermore,
The river grows out like a tree.

An empty page and a little luck

I am staring a blank page hoping for good words to pour out,
everthing is in order so I use all my verbal clout,
and hope for more words to appear on the page,
going well I feel more confident and act like a sage,
I lose myself in the words and out pops a line unexpected,
a good phrase so good so clever I could hardly expect.

RACHEL LAWSON

A Shower of Meteors

Bewitched by her silvery glow:
I stand
alone
in silence
with bated breath,
enchanted by a cool—
clear starlit night of beauty,
gazing into a dark glowing sky
thinking of fair Luna
in her beauty
in a shower of lights
falling from skies above
a meteoric rain of fire.

Drops of Jupiter

I am consumed in beauty like liquid drops of Jupiter,
Mercury surrounds its essence is like a pure liqueur,
heady and light like the quintessence of purest Sunlight,
with darkness as black as the dark side of a Plutonian night,
solid as the Earth's rocky surface,
sparkling like the celestial travelers of deep space,
raining like fountains of falling stars,
entwined with the purest love of Venus and Mars.

RACHEL LAWSON

The Water Lilly

Upon a still pond, floats a perfect jewel of snow,
from it, green plate-like leaves did grow,
upon it sat a lethargic frog trying to catch a sultry fly,
a fish in depths swimming beyond the human eye,
a slight breeze causes the water to ripple and wane,
the lily nodded to the waters soothing refrain.

The Windswept Streets

The air is crisp and breezy,
the leaves fly easy,
they tumble in the air,
but few even care,
the trees sway,
It's been like this all day,
the wind wails a lament which is it's alone,
buildings creak as they are blown,
I too am blown from behind,
by the east wind,
in its fury, it rustles my hair and clothes and it repeats
I spy a newspaper fluttering down the windswept streets.

RACHEL LAWSON

The Ocean

The water gently laps upon the shore
with a cheery swish of water hitting the sand,
it bears a magical air of relaxation,
to the listener's ear mind and soul.

Everybody dreams

Everybody sees things differently,
one may see the work of man,
another may see the work of nature,
it is called perspective.

Ghostwriters In The Sky

I was wandering through a desert hot,
In the sky, I saw people writing a lot,
one called my name and said be careful or you may share our fate,
"what fate what are you doing?" I asked
"we are ghostwriters to write in the sky we are tasked,"
"what!" I cried,
"how do I write my way out of that!" the ghostwriter said I don't think
he lied
I was sure I was hallucinating.
"who you ghostwriting for?"
"God we ghostwrite for"
"god?" I said, my god I thought I was stark raving mad.
I had to get out of the desert or die so no time for them I had,
"go away! let me go mad on my own,'
I didn't believe what I was shown.

The End

95

Don't miss out!

Visit the website below and you can sign up to receive emails whenever Rachel Lawson publishes a new book. There's no charge and no obligation.

https://books2read.com/r/B-A-HMGO-CPNTB

BOOKS 2 READ

Connecting independent readers to independent writers.

9 798201 957001